MCWP 4-11.8

Services in an Expeditionary Environment

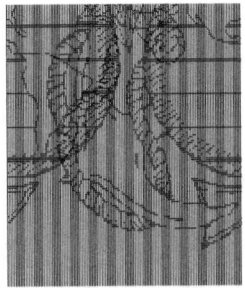

U.S. Marine Corps

To Our Readers

Changes: Readers of this publication are encouraged to submit suggestions and changes that will improve it. Recommendations may be sent directly to Commanding General, Marine Corps Combat Development Command, Doctrine Division (C 42), 3300 Russell Road, Suite 318A, Quantico, VA 22134-5021 or by fax to 703-784-2917 (DSN 278-2917) or by E-mail to **morgann@mccdc.usmc.mil**. Recommendations should include the following information:

- Location of change
  Publication number and title
  Current page number
  Paragraph number (if applicable)
  Line number
  Figure or table number (if applicable)
- Nature of change
  Add, delete
  Proposed new text, preferably double-spaced and typewritten
- Justification and/or source of change

Additional copies: A printed copy of this publication may be obtained from Marine Corps Logistics Base, Albany, GA 31704-5001, by following the instructions in MCBul 5600, *Marine Corps Doctrinal Publications Status.* An electronic copy may be obtained from the Doctrine Division, MCCDC, world wide web home page which is found at the following universal reference locator: **http://www.doctrine.usmc.mil**.

Unless otherwise stated, whenever the masculine gender is used, both men and women are included.

DEPARTMENT OF THE NAVY
Headquarters United States Marine Corps
Washington, D.C. 20380-1775

24 September 2001

FOREWORD

PURPOSE

Marine Corps Warfighting Publication (MCWP) 4-11.8, *Services in an Expeditionary Environment*, provides the doctrinal basis for the planning and execution of services at the operational and tactical levels of war. It establishes terms of reference for combat service support services and provides guidance to Marine Forces in the development of local standing operating procedures in an expeditionary environment.

SCOPE

MCWP 4-11.8 identifies the command support services inherent in every command and the services specifically provided by the Marine air-ground task force (MAGTF) combat service support element. Specifically, this publication focuses on the functions, organization, and staff cognizance of services in an expeditionary environment. It provides guidance and serves as a reference tool for all commanders, logisticians, and staff planners.

SUPERSESSION

None.

CERTIFICATION

Reviewed and approved this date.

BY DIRECTION OF THE COMMANDANT OF THE
MARINE CORPS

/s/
EDWARD HANLON, JR.
Lieutenant General, U.S. Marine Corps
Commanding General
Marine Corps Combat Development Command
Quantico, Virginia

DISTRIBUTION: 143 000089 00

Services in an Expeditionary Environment

Table of Contents

Chapter 1. Services Overview

Chapter 2. Postal Services

Chapter 3. Legal Services

Chapter 4. Mortuary Affairs Services

Chapter 5. Field Exchange Services

Chapter 6. Security Support Services

Chapter 7. Disbursing Services

Chapter 8. Civil-Military Operations Services

Appendices

Chapter 1
Services Overview

Services are those activities that are necessary for the effective administration, management, and employment of military organizations. The subfunctions of services are essentially administrative or nonmateriel in nature and are implemented with uniform systems and procedures. Services are either a function of command support or combat service support. Services that are command support include activities that are inherent in every command (e.g., personnel administration, billeting). Services that are combat service support include services not normally available in or organic to all elements of the Marine air-ground task force (MAGTF) and are provided by the combat service support element (CSSE) (e.g., mortuary affairs, exchange services). Many services are performed by specialists (special staff officers) who report directly to the MAGTF commander or other principal staff officers, not to the G-4/S-4 (logistic officer).

Services that are a function of command support normally reside within the headquarters and service (H&S) battalions of the MAGTF ground combat element (GCE), aviation combat element (ACE), and CSSE companies. These services include personnel administration; religious ministry; billeting; financial management; morale, welfare, and recreation; and messing. Messing, currently a command support function, may become the responsibility of the CSSE. See Marine Corps Reference Publication (MCRP) 4-11.8A, *Food Services Reference*, for more information.

Services that are a function of combat service support and the responsibility of the CSSE include postal, legal, mortuary affairs (graves registration), exchange, security support, disbursing, and civil-military operations (CMO). Typically, the force service support group (FSSG) provides these services to the elements of the Marine expeditionary force (MEF).

Joint Publication (JP) 4-0, *Doctrine for Logistic Support of Joint Operations*; Naval Doctrine Publication (NDP) 4, *Naval Logistics*; and Marine Corps Doctrinal Publication (MCDP) 4, *Logistics*, discuss a variety of nonmateriel and support activities that are identified as services. These services are executed in varying degrees by each of the military Services, the Marine Corps supporting establishment, and the MAGTF. An understanding of the division of labor and interrelationship of the responsibilities and staff cognizance for specific services is essential to effectively accomplish services as a function.

Organizations

MEF Headquarters Group

The MEF headquarters group provides administrative and services support to the MEF command element. It also provides administrative and services support to intelligence, counterintelligence, ground reconnaissance, communications, and information systems and to liaison organizations subordinate to the MEF. Additionally, it provides headquarters commandant support to the MEF command element.

Headquarters Battalion, Marine Division

Within the Marine division, the H&S and military police (MP) companies of the headquarters battalion are principally responsible for services. The H&S company provides command, administrative, and security functions, as well as organic supply and food service for the headquarters battalion. The MP company provides route reconnaissance, evacuation and control of enemy prisoners of war (EPW), beach and perimeter defense, area security, crowd control, and investigative services for the division.

Marine Wing Headquarters Squadron

The Marine wing headquarters squadron provides command, administrative, and supply support for a Marine aircraft wing headquarters and certain elements of the Marine air control group. It provides camp facilities and services, including food service, for all elements of the Marine wing headquarters, for the Marine tactical air command squadron, and for the Marine wing communications squadron of the Marine air control group. The Marine wing headquarters squadron maintains the capability of deploying as an integral unit when augmented with maintenance support personnel. It provides detachments for supported units as required. It also provides for internal security of the Marine aircraft wing headquarters.

Headquarters and Service Battalion, FSSG

The H&S battalion provides command and control, administrative, services, communications, and security support to the FSSG and coordination of services support beyond supported unit organic capabilities to the MAGTF. The battalion is self-supporting in organic supply, organizational maintenance, health services, communications, and transportation for its command and administrative functions. In addition, the battalion provides communications for the command elements of the FSSG and subordinate combat service support detachments, and messing for itself and maintenance, supply, and motor transport battalions. The

H&S battalion is organized into headquarters, MP, services, and communications companies. The service company and the MP company provide external services in support of the MAGTF.

Service Company

The service company provides general support services to the MEF and administrative and disbursing support to U.S. Navy personnel assigned to the MEF. It contains the following functional units:

- Company headquarters, which includes a nucleus of initial, active-duty civil affairs support for the MEF when augmented by the civil affairs group (CAG) attached from the Reserves.
- Graves registration platoon, if activated from the Reserves, is normally attached.
- MEF postal platoon.
- Legal support section.
- Disbursing platoon.
- MEF exchange platoon.
- Information system management unit.
- Naval personnel support section.

MP Company

The MP company provides security support to the FSSG, the MEF, and the MAGTF. It also provides battlespace circulation control, area security, EPW control, and law and order operations. The MP company can transport its administrative and command functions and performs organizational maintenance on organic equipment. It contains a company headquarters and three MP platoons.

Staff Cognizance

Centralization of many of the services capabilities within the FSSG does not infer sole logistic staff cognizance for execution of the task. For example, disbursing, postal, and legal services are task-organized to support all elements of the MEF, and their function is executed under the cognizance of the supported element personnel officer (G-1/S-1) and the MAGTF commander, not the logistic officer (G-4/S-4). Security support is an operational concern reflecting potential rear area security missions that the rear area commander might assign to the MP company, although each element of the MEF possesses an organic MP capability and could be similarly tasked. CMO and mortuary affairs services are limited to units in the Reserve establishment (4th FSSG) that are assisted by logistic capabilities and augmented by other military Services units. Exchange and CMO services require management and distribution of class VI and class X supply items, which are held by the supply battalion, FSSG. However, the execution of CMO is typically an operational concern. Mortuary affairs services are fully integrated with the G-1/S-1 for casualty reporting and notification. Support of both CMO and mortuary affairs is a shared responsibility and depends on the augmentation capabilities external to the MEF.

Command Support Services

Command support services are those services inherent to any command. They are typically executed without augmentation by external agencies or organizations. These services include personnel administration; religious ministry; billeting; financial management; morale, welfare, and recreation; and messing.

Personnel Administration

Personnel administration is a function of the G-1/S-1 and entails the normal personnel administrative matters and requirements of normal day-to-day unit operation. The G-1/S-1 is also responsible for other personnel-related issues and functions within the MAGTF.

The G-1/S-1 estimates the number of personnel required to maintain operational strength. This includes estimates of the personnel required to complete the mission and loss estimates/replacements. Tentative personnel plans are issued to subordinate and interested commands for concurrent planning. The G-1/S-1 also recommends solutions to personnel requirements of any unit that is to be added to the task organization; e.g., MP or graves registration personnel. Strength estimates are also used to assist in the overall development of transportation requirements. For example, estimates would address the transportation requirements needed to support graves registration, process EPWs, treat and evacuate the wounded, and relocate installations to temporary sites.

Personnel losses are classified as either administrative losses, nonbattle casualties, or battle casualties. Administrative losses include transfers, unauthorized absences, and rotational losses; they do not result from wounds, injuries or diseases. Nonbattle casualties are all other casualties not associated with a combat mission. A battle casualty is any Marine lost to the mission; i.e., killed in action, died of wounds and injuries received in action, wounded or injured in action, missing in action, or captured by the enemy.

The G-1/S-1 is also responsible for other personnel functions and takes the lead in coordinating mortuary affairs/graves registration; handling EPWs; civilian personnel matters (contractors, civilian employees, and refugees, etc.); interior management, and discipline, law, and order.

Religious Ministry

Religious ministry performs ecclesiastic functions and provides both faith-based and nondenominational counseling and guidance for all personnel. It is a significant factor in building and maintaining morale. Chaplains are assigned throughout the MAGTF at the organizational level and higher. Chaplains normally report directly to the commander. Marine Corps Warfighting Publication (MCWP) 6-12, *Religious Ministry Support in the USMC*, and MCRPs in the 6-12 series address religious ministry in detail.

Billeting

Billeting is the availability of safe and sanitary living quarters, commensurate with operational circumstances, for assigned personnel. Billeting options span a wide spectrum, from comfortable family housing and motel-like bachelor quarters in garrison, to crowded shipboard berthing compartments, to group and/or two-man tents in the field, to rough bunkers and fighting holes in combat. Providing proper billeting is a command responsibility that organizational commanders exercise through subordinate unit leaders. The commander's logistic officer (G-4/S-4) normally has staff cognizance of facilities support for billeting.

Financial Management

Financial management is inseparable from command. The commander must make vital fiscal decisions and keep financial management in proper perspective as part of balanced staff actions. The commander must recognize that financial management has no bearing on the determination of the mission, but rather it is a primary consideration in determining both the means and the time phasing of mission accomplishment.

The commander has two types of financial responsibility: command and legal. Command responsibility parallels the commander's other responsibilities and tasks him with the control and administration of funds granted to perform the mission. Legal responsibility is the requirement not to over commit, over obligate, or over expend appropriated funds when the commander is in receipt of an allotment or operating budget.

Financial management operations within the operating forces may be divided into four fundamental areas: budgeting, accounting, disbursing, and auditing. To assist the commander in the accomplishment of these functions, a comptroller is established at each major command. Commanders at lower echelons normally assign the additional duty of fiscal officer to a special staff officer (e.g., the supply officer) or an organizational staff officer (e.g., the S-4). The comptroller (or fiscal officer) acts as the principal financial advisor to the commander.

Morale, Welfare, and Recreation

Morale, welfare, and recreation activities are generally "off-duty" opportunities that relax and relieve the stress and tediousness of military operations. Morale, welfare, and recreation are managed through command channels, but funding and support start at the unit level. Movies, live entertainment shows, and unit-level parties are examples of morale, welfare, and recreation events. Reasonable morale, welfare, and recreation activities are desirable, particularly in austere expeditionary settings, but they are never considered essential if they interfere with mission accomplishment.

Messing

Messing, or food service, is the provision of nutritional meals to personnel. It also includes subsistence accounting, management, and operation of dining facilities that prepare and serve food. Organizational subsistence responsibilities include accounting for all subsistence from the time of receipt until the time of consumption, including refrigerated and nonrefrigerated storage.

The employment of food service resources is situation dependent, and their centralized or decentralized employment is the subject of planning by the G-4/S-4 in coordination with food service officers, dining facility managers, and the CSSE commander. During combat operations, food service resources may need to be centralized within the MAGTF. This is particularly true when planning for the provision of such food service items as baked goods and A or B ration preparation and distribution tasks. Decentralizing food service resources down to the company/battery levels may be appropriate under certain conditions. Ration consumption and distribution methods are determined by unit missions; weights and quantities of rations; troop strengths; operational environment; and climate.

CSSE Services

The CSSE provides services not available in or organic to other MAGTF elements. These services include postal, legal, mortuary affairs, field exchange, security, disbursing, and CMO.

Postal Services

Postal assets are task-organized to provide postal support to the MAGTF and attachments. These assets include 1 mobile main post office and up to 12 mobile unit post offices. Each mobile unit post office is capable of providing full postal support to a reinforced regiment. The main post office coordinates all postal functions and locations.

The bulk of postal support will be located throughout the MAGTF rear area. Mobile unit post offices will provide postal support to combat service support areas located in the force combat service support area. On request from the GCE, mobile unit post offices may be located in the GCE rear area. These mobile units provide full or partial postal services as required. The ACE is provided postal services through the use of mobile unit post offices. If postal services are not requested by the GCE or ACE, the delivery of mail to personnel in the GCE's front line forces or in the ACE is accomplished through resupply channels. All postal units respond to the tasking of their respective area commanders, but they receive procedural direction from the MAGTF postal officer who is solely responsible for all postal operations. Chapter 2 has more information on postal services.

Legal Services

The legal services support section (LSSS), H&S battalion, FSSG is the command entity that provides legal services support to the MAGTF. Legal services involve command advice; supply, injury, or death investigation, advice, and review; claims processing; legal review of operation plans; law of war training; legal assistance; administrative separations processing; nonjudicial punishment (NJP) advice; and summary, special, and general court-martial processing.

LSSS and legal services support teams (LSSTs) are employed at appropriate times and places to support personnel in the MAGTF area of operations. LSSTs may vary in number, size, and composition depending on the mission, size, and composition of the MAGTF; expected duration of the operation; and the scheme of maneuver and topography of the operation. Chapter 3 has more information on legal services.

Mortuary Affairs Services

Mortuary affairs services require specialized capabilities, which are beyond the capabilities of the MAGTF. The U.S. Army provides these mortuary affairs services for the Department of Defense. However, during MAGTF operations, mortuary affairs operations consist of search, recovery, and identification of deceased personnel and the final disposition of their personal property. Formal chains of evacuation and accountability begin at the unit level; therefore, every small-unit leader and commander is responsible for mortuary affairs. Battalions establish casualty collection teams and collection points. Collection points are normally collocated with aid stations, but mortuary affairs operations and health services operations are distinctly separate operations. Chapter 4 has more information on mortuary affairs services.

Field Exchange Services

During deployment, exchange services are provided by a tactical field exchange, which is established when no other source of class VI support is available. The MAGTF commander determines the need to establish a tactical field exchange. The CSSE commander determines the location of the tactical field exchange in accordance with guidance established by the MAGTF commander. A mobile tactical field exchange is part of the tactical field exchange and provides exchange services to MAGTF maneuver elements as needed. Chapter 5 has more information on field exchange services.

Security Support Services

Primarily, the MP company, H&S battalion, FSSG provides security support to the MAGTF. The MP company's table of organization (T/O) precludes it from providing all security support functions simultaneously; therefore, assets must be used wisely. The MP company supports the MAGTF by providing battlefield circulation control, area security, EPW management, and law and order. Chapter 6 has more information on security support services.

Disbursing Services

CSSE disbursing assets can deploy to provide full service disbursing support to the rest of the MAGTF. These services include, but are not limited to, claims, currency exchange, personnel pay, and check cashing. MAGTF disbursing support should be located in the CSSE rear area. These offices will respond to the tasking of their respective commanders, but will receive procedural direction from the MAGTF disbursing officer who is solely responsible for all disbursing operations. Chapter 7 has more information on disbursing services.

Civil-Military Operations Services

CMO is a command responsibility. Civil affairs units, which reside in the Reserves, are normally assigned to the MAGTF command element and function under the cognizance of the MAGTF G-3/S-3. They assist in planning, conducting, and implementing MAGTF CMO and coordinating and managing civil-military activities that support MAGTF operations. Chapter 8 contains more information on CMO.

Chapter 2
Postal Services

The timely delivery of personal mail is a critical element in maintaining individual and unit morale, which directly affects the combat readiness and effectiveness of individual Marines. Depending on the operating environment, a Marine's access to telephone services may be limited and letters and packages may be his only means of continued communications with his separated family.

In an expeditionary environment, the MAGTF commander is responsible for postal services within the MAGTF's area of operations and determines the need for a military postal office. The need for a military postal office is based on the duration and location of the deployment. If a military postal office is established, the MAGTF commander appoints a postal officer to handle all postal services for the MAGTF.

The military postal office's functions include processing personal, official, and free mail. Personal mail is addressed to or sent by individuals for personal use. Official mail is addressed to or sent by the unit and is necessary to operate the unit. The MAGTF commander establishes guidance for the use of free mail. Free mail is mail processed without postage while in theater. Free mail also includes mail that never comes in contact with a commercial postal facility; it is routed through military postal offices bearing the letters MPS (military postal service) in place of a stamp.

The military post office also provides such civilian postal services as selling stamps and weighing packages. The military post office complies with Department of Defense (DOD) 4525.6M, *DOD Postal Manual*, volumes I and II.

Planning Requirements

The postal officer identifies postal requirements and determines and plans postal services for the MAGTF. These services include, but are not limited to, the following:

- Establishing procedures to provide mail support within the area of operations.
- Identifying transportation requirements for mail within the area of operations.
- Identifying personnel requirements in order to staff both main and satellite military postal offices. The supported unit's/MAGTF's size, type of postal services required, geographic location of the supported unit/MAGTF, and availability of existing postal services determine personnel requirements.
- Determining postal and administrative equipment requirements needed to support postal operations.
- Identifying addresses for both personal and official mail.
- Establishing mail accounting procedures (i.e., receiving, dispatching, and securing).
- Identifying directory instructions, to include home station and deploying units' information.
- Establishing a casualty mail section.
- Identifying routing and disposition instructions.
- Identifying postal assets available within the area of operations in order to prevent duplication of services.
- Determining resupply of postal stock.
- Identifying postal restrictions.

- Determining if free mail is authorized within the theater.

- Identifying postal command relationships, to include Department of Defense, Military Postal Services Agency.

- Determining if inspections and audits of the postal facility and mail handling procedures will be suspended.

- Establishing an evacuation plan for mail in the event the postal facility is overtaken or there is an immediate threat requiring permanent or temporary movement of the postal facility.

- Developing procedures to handle and hold contaminated mail and accountable mail.

- Developing a plan for mail that cannot be delivered, commonly referred to as retrograde mail.

- Identifying unit sort requirements and providing them to the appropriate Joint Military Postal Activity.

- Identifying military postal services to noncombatant evacuation operations (NEO) prior to departure of affected personnel.

- Coordinating with the J-1 postal staff if the MAGTF is part of a joint forces command to determine if a single service manager has been designated. The postal officer coordinates with the single service manager or designated authority to—

  - Coordinate the dissemination of address information, mailing information, and mailing restrictions.

  - Determine zip assignments and sorting levels, restrictions and lift capabilities, and routing and opening dates for start of mail flow.

  - Identify coalition and North Atlantic Treaty Organization (NATO) forces postal requirements.

  - Determine the use of free mail.

Postal services occur in three phases (see table 2-1). Phase 1 includes the establishment of an initial secure area and postal services are not provided. Phase 2 begins once a secure area is established. During phase 2, the military postal office is assigned facilities and equipment to begin processing mail and to begin operation of a finance unit. Initially, military postal office operations are limited. The assignment of personnel and equipment determines how rapidly the military postal office can offer full postal services. The military postal office moves into phase 3 once all postal assets are received and committed in support of the postal mission.

Free Mail

Free mail must weigh 11 ounces or less and is limited to First Class letter mail or to sound recorded communications that replicate personal correspondence. Free mail is a privilege. It is authorized for members of the U.S. Armed Forces on duty in combat areas specifically designated by the Secretary of Defense. It also applies to persons who are no longer in a combat area but are hospitalized in any Armed Forces or Veterans Administration medical center due to a wound, disease or other injury incident. The Military Postal Services Agency publishes detailed instructions on implementation of free mail within each area of responsibility.

Casualty Mail Handling

The casualty mail section will maintain directory files on personnel reported as deceased, hospitalized, missing, captured, or interned. The hospital mail section will maintain directory files on admitted patients and evacuees. Mail for casualties shall not

Table 2-1. Phases of Postal Services.

Support Provided	Phase 1	Phase 2	Phase 3
Mail receipt, distribution, and dispatch.		●	●
Finance support.		●	●
Restricted mail service.		●	●
Advising the MAGTF commander on postal matters.	●	●	●
Establishing the military postal office.			●
Establishing unit post office(s).		●	●
Establishing the mail directory and casualty mail section.		●	●
Coordinating internal and external area of operations mail routing.		●	●
Providing finance services, to include stamp, envelope, postcard, and money order sales.			●
Providing United States Postal Service money order cashing capability.			●
Providing acceptance, sorting, and distribution of official and personal mail.			●
Establishing resupply of post office supplies and accountable postal stocks (e.g., stamps, money orders).			●
Coordinating cross-service support as required.			●

be returned or forwarded to the next of kin until verification is obtained that the next of kin has been notified. Mail will be held as long as necessary to prevent inadvertent disclosure before official notification. Once notification is confirmed, the mail will be returned to the sender or forwarded to the next of kin with a cover letter attached. Verification can be obtained from the service headquarters of the following:

- Marine Corps' casualty mail section.
- Navy's command element.
- Army's casualty mail section.
- Air Force's summary court officer.

Enemy Prisoner of War Mail Handling

The Geneva Convention of 1949 established mail handling procedures for EPWs. Under the auspices of the Geneva Convention, countries involved in conflicts will negotiate the details for the handling, transporting, and exchanging of mail. The Geneva Convention identifies the International Committee of the Red Cross as coordinator for these negotiations, and the United States designates the Department of State as its representative. The negotiated results may have military postal service implications, so the Military Postal Services Agency must plan for handling the mail.

Due to the uncertainty of conditions within the MAGTF area of operations, the Military Postal Services Agency will disseminate instructions to the military postal service element responsible for handling EPW mail. The military postal service element shall ensure that transportation and routing requirements are established and that detainee mail transits the military postal service in closed pouches. The military postal service element will inspect operations at EPW sites to ensure compliance with proper mail handling procedures. The military postal service element will not recognize special services (i.e., registered, certified, or cash on delivery [COD]) mail for or from detainees. The military postal service element will maintain close liaison with commanders operating EPW facilities concerning detainee mail. Commanders operating EPW facilities will establish mailrooms, designate mail clerks or orderlies per DOD 4525.6M (volume II), and ensure that mail clerks/orderlies are properly trained.

Chapter 3
Legal Services

The political and legal complexities of the modern world can significantly affect military operations. Marine Corps commanders, whether in garrison or deployed, are confronted on a daily basis with complex, technical military justice and administrative law issues. International law, treaties, status of forces agreements, Law of War, Code of Conduct, claims, and other issues directly impact Marine Corps operations. Legal services are task-organized to address a command's legal needs both in garrison and throughout the deployable spectrum of conflict—from domestic disaster relief operations to major regional contingencies. Therefore, professional and comprehensive legal services are provided at virtually every level of command, and Marines and civilian personnel trained in legal matters are positioned throughout the operating forces and supporting establishment. This chapter addresses legal services that are dedicated to the operating forces. Many legal services and organizational structures discussed is this chapter are also applicable to forces in garrison, base and station operations, and the Reserves.

Organization

The commanding general, FSSG is responsible to the commanding general, MEF for providing the full range of military justice, administrative law, operational law, and legal assistance support to all supported commands. The commanding general, FSSG exercises this responsibility through the officer in charge, LSSS, service company, H&S battalion, FSSG. Legal services consist of two major parts: staff judge advocates who directly represent the commanders; and judge advocates who represent servicemembers, their families, and retirees.

Staff Judge Advocate

The staff judge advocate (SJA) (senior judge advocate in commands not having general court-martial authority) is the command's principal legal advisor and a member of the commander's special staff. The MEF, each major subordinate command of the MEF, most special purpose MAGTFs, and each base or station within the supporting establishment are assigned an SJA. If a subordinate command does not have an SJA, then an SJA from a senior command will be assigned to the subordinate command to provide legal support. Each Marine Corps commanding general receives direct legal advice on all pertinent legal issues from the command's SJA, and commanders at all levels should consult with the SJA on all legal matters that affect the command.

Legal Services Support Section

The LSSS operates under the direction of an officer in charge, who is an experienced attorney (judge advocate). The officer in charge is a special staff officer to the commanding general, FSSG and is responsible to the commanding general, FSSG through the chief of staff. The LSSS officer in charge coordinates actions with all supported command SJAs. The officer in charge must provide timely, periodic reports to all the supported SJAs regarding assignments, courts-martial processing, administrative discharge boards, courts-reporting, and case reviews. The LSSS is fully deployable and has an approved T/O and table of equipment (T/E) within service company, H&S battalion, FSSG. Subordinate LSSTs are formed as needed at the direction of the LSSS officer in charge. They are task-organized from LSSS assets to support specific legal services.

Mission and Responsibilities

Staff Judge Advocate

At every level, the SJA acts as the primary legal advisor to the respective commander, commanding general, commanding officer, subordinate commander, or staff members. The SJA provides advice and assistance on the entire range of legal issues confronting the command. These include, but are not limited to the following:

- All aspects of military justice.
- Administrative separations.
- Administrative investigations.
- Claims.
- Civil litigation affecting the command.
- Civil-military relations.
- Domestic law that affects military operations.
- Legal assistance.
- Labor law.
- Environmental law.
- Operational and international law.
- Coordination with the LSSS officer in charge for appropriate legal services (except in Marine Corps Forces Reserve).

Legal Services Support Section

The commanding general, FSSG (except 4th FSSG) is responsible for providing legal services to the MEF. This responsibility is exercised through the LSSS and any subordinate LSSTs. By efficiently organizing legal personnel and resources, the officer in charge ensures that the LSSS provides all supported commands with the full range of legal services, whether in garrison or during MAGTF operations, in a timely and effective manner. This support includes all administrative, technical, and personnel aspects of the following:

- Military justice, particularly in regard to the entire court-martial and initial appellate review process.
- Defense counsel services.
- Coordination with criminal investigative agencies.
- Review of criminal investigations.
- NJP counseling and review of NJP appeals.
- Involuntary administrative separations.
- Training of and assistance to those conducting litigation reports and command-directed informal investigations in accordance with the JAGInst 5800.7c, *The Manual of the Judge Advocate General (JAGMAN)*, which contains rules and regulations governing members of the armed forces.
- Review of reports of investigations.
- Legal assistance.
- Foreign civil or criminal jurisdiction over servicemembers.
- Legal research (limited during MAGTF operations).
- Training of unit legal officers.
- Operational and international law, particularly unit training on Law of War, Code of Conduct, rules of engagement, and status of forces agreements.
- Operational and training exercise support.
- Assisting the MAGTF with processing and treatment of EPWs.

- Claims processing.

- Providing the MAGTF with limited, interim CMO capability.

Each LSSS will contain the following component sections; section functions may differ slightly between each LSSS.

Officer in Charge Section

The officer in charge section consists of the officer in charge, an assistant officer in charge, a legal administrative officer, a legal services chief, and other personnel as needed. The officer in charge is responsible for the performance of all legal services of the LSSS and subordinate LSSTs. The legal administrative officer performs fiscal and accounting functions; coordinates continuing legal education training and requirements; coordinates internal supply and property accounting; manages research and library resources and automated data processing equipment, including maintenance and software contracts; and coordinates logistical support/embarkation requirements. The legal services chief is the senior enlisted advisor to the officer in charge and coordinates all enlisted functions and assignments within the LSSS.

Administrative Support Section

The administrative support section normally consists of an administrative support chief and one or more legal clerks. This section provides clerical support to the officer in charge section and general administrative support to the entire LSSS. This support includes processing of temporary additional duty requests, fitness reports, leave requests, external record of trial, guard mail distribution management, computer support, local area network administration, information systems and database management, and publications and library services.

Military Justice Section

The military justice section consists of a military justice officer, senior trial counsel, military justice chief, one or more trial counsels, and one or more legal clerks. The military justice section represents the U.S. Government in all special and general courts-martial and involuntary administrative separation proceedings. This section performs and coordinates all required pre-trial, trial, and post-trial actions from receipt of a Request for Legal Services (RLS) form to authentication of completed records of trial.

Defense Section

The defense section consists of a senior defense counsel, one or more defense counsels, and one or more legal clerks. The defense section provides legal advice and representation to servicemembers accused of Unified Code of Military Justice violations. It provides defense counsel to represent servicemembers before special and general courts-martial, involuntary administrative separation proceedings, and initial review officer pre-trial confinement hearings. This section also provides advice regarding NJP; other adverse disciplinary matters; and constitutional, statutory, and regulatory rights of individual servicemembers. Defense counsel is responsible to the LSSS officer in charge for administrative purposes only (e.g., duty hours, formations, physical training). In matters related to its duties as defense counsel, defense counsel receives supervision/guidance and fitness reports from the senior or regional defense counsel.

Court Reporter Section

The court reporter section consists of a court reporter chief, one or more court reporters, and one or more court recorders. This section provides summarized or verbatim records of trial for all special and general courts-martial, and verbatim records of other military justice-related proceedings and administrative proceedings (e.g., Article 32 investigations, officer NJPs, boards of inquiry). Scopists, with computer assistance, transcribe stenographic court reporter notes into English-language text.

Review Section

The review section consists of a chief review officer, one or more judge advocates, a review chief, and one or more legal clerks. This section performs post-trial review and processing of all courts-martial (including cases returned after appellate review), review of NJP appeals, preparation of post-trial documents for SJAs and convening authorities, maintenance of records of trial, and forwarding of records of trial to the appropriate appellate authorities.

Administrative Law Section

The administrative law section consists of an administrative law officer, an administrative law chief, one or more legal clerks, and if possible, one or more non-lawyer officers as administrative discharge board recorders. This section reviews administrative investigations and preliminary inquiries and claims against the U.S. Government. This section processes all involuntary administrative separations in which judge advocate counseling, representation, or review is required by law or regulation. Administrative discharge board recorders, other than the administrative law officer or trial counsel, may be junior officers provided through the Fleet Assistance Program to represent the U.S. Government in discharge board proceedings in order to ensure fundamental fairness to the respondent in such proceedings.

Operational Law Section

The operational law section consists of one or more judge advocates and minimal clerical support. This section fulfills MEF requirements for training, exercise, and contingency operation support and provides training and research capabilities to supported commands regarding international law, treaties, other international agreements, Law of War, EPW handling, Code of Conduct, rules of engagement, CMO, trial observer/reporting services for foreign trials involving servicemembers, and other similar services requiring a legal liaison with foreign governments. The operational law section provides training and research capabilities for domestic operations and exercises, including consequence management/weapons of mass destruction, homeland defense, domestic disaster assistance, civil disturbance operations, and military support to civil authorities.

Legal Assistance Section

The legal assistance section consists of one or more judge advocates and one or more legal clerks. This section provides counseling to individual servicemembers regarding taxes, wills, powers of attorney, family law, contract law, consumer protection, and a wide variety of civil law issues. It also provides unit-wide predeployment training on these issues. In garrison, this section may be supported by the base SJA or consolidated legal assistance office.

Planning

When planning legal services, the commander's staff considers the following factors:

- Current situation.

- Mission of the supported unit(s).

- Size, type, and location of the supported unit(s).

- Size, location, and geography of the area of operations.

- Communications.

- Computer support.

- General logistic support.

- Vehicular support.

- Numbers and military occupational specialties (MOSs) of available legal services personnel.

- Research assets.

- Command relationships.

- Coordination with supported units' SJA(s).

During MAGTF operations, in addition to the normal planning factors listed above, the following must also be considered:

- Amount of available planning time.

- The operation plan and commander's intent.

- The supported units' scheme(s) of maneuver.

- Time-phased force and deployment data.

- Any applicable status of forces agreement.

- Other treaties or agreements in force.

- Host nation criminal and civil jurisdiction over U.S. military personnel if not addressed in existing agreements.

- Availability of host nation support.

- Rules of engagement (i.e., development, dissemination, and training).

- EPWs.

- Presence of civilians in area of operation.

- Liberty areas within the area of operation.

- Need for a confinement facility.

- Role of the MAGTF in administrative claims adjudication.

- Availability of other judge advocate support (e.g., joint task force or commander in chief).

Requests for Support

Timely, professional legal services will be readily available to all commands and servicemembers. However, legal services operations must be understood in terms of their connection within the supporting/supported command relationship. The statutory and regulatory roles and responsibilities of the convening authority, reviewing authority, administrative separation authority, and SJA are not altered by the existence of the LSSS.

The LSSS/LSST will handle as much legal administration for supported commands as possible. Supported commands submit an RLS form to request support for military justice or administrative separation from the supporting LSSS/LSST. The RLS should be accompanied by documents relevant to the request, such as reports of investigation, witness statements, etc. The RLS and other legal forms will be as simple, easy to use, standardized, and readily available to supported commands as possible. Requests for any other type of legal support provided by the LSSS/LSST can be made informally.

Chapter 4
Mortuary Affairs Services

As stated in JP 4-06, *Joint Tactics, Techniques, and Procedures for Mortuary Affairs in Joint Operations*, the remains of all members of the Armed Forces will be returned for permanent disposition according to the direction of the person authorized to direct disposition of remains. Mortuary affairs is the recovery of remains and personal effects, identification of remains, and evacuation of remains to a temporary cemetery within the theater for burial or to a mortuary facility. Mortuary affairs consists of three different programs: current death program, concurrent return program, and graves registration program. Each program occurs at distinct stages.

Mortuary Affairs Programs

Current Death Program

The current death program is in effect during peacetime and during hostilities of short duration when few casualties are expected. Remains are moved from a unit's area of operation to a collection point, then to a mortuary either within or outside the continental United States, and finally to the person authorized to direct disposition of remains.

Concurrent Return Program

The concurrent return program is in effect during wartime. Under this program, remains move from the unit area of operation to a collection point, then to a Theater Mortuary Evacuation Point (TMEP), next to a mortuary located in the continental United States, and finally to the person authorized to direct disposition of remains.

Graves Registration Program

The graves registration program is used only as a last resort and only upon order of the geographic combatant commander. This program is only enacted when an overwhelming number of remains prevents normal mortuary affairs operations from occurring or when contaminated remains cannot be decontaminated. Graves registration program objectives include the following:

- Sustained troop morale.
- Search for and attempted recovery of remains.
- Prompt, accurate identification of remains.
- Evacuation of remains.
- Prompt recovery, inventory, and shipment of personal effects.
- Prompt, accurate, and complete administrative recording and reporting.
- Prompt, adequate care for deceased allies and enemy personnel.

Organization

The Army is the executive agent of mortuary affairs for all Services. However, each Service plays a major role in the handling of its deceased. In the Marine Corps, mortuary affairs responsibilities reside in the Reserves, whose primary focus is graves registration. The reserve unit is the Graves Registration Platoon, H&S Company, H&S Battalion, 4th FSSG. The graves registration platoon's T/O consists of 1 Marine officer, 42 Marines, and 3 enlisted Navy embalmers. The platoon conducts tactical search and recovery operations in hostile, benign, and/or contaminated environments; recovers personal effects and records personal information; conducts temporary interment/disinterment; and conducts temporary burials, if necessary, of human remains. The platoon must also be prepared to establish and operate casualty collection points, supervise theater evacuation point operations, and coordinate the transfer of remains and personal effects of deceased servicemembers.

Mortuary Affairs Collection Point

A Mortuary Affairs Collection Point (MACP) is a designated site where specially-trained personnel provide technical assistance for the acceptance and disposition of remains. This includes interment, interment records, and temporary interment site maintenance until other provisions are made for subsequent custody/disposition. The MACP is an intermediate or transit point for remains.

The MAGTF commander chooses the site of the MACP. When selecting a site, it should be close to a main supply route, have easy access to a landing strip or fixed airport, and be located on terrain that accommodates a temporary interment site.

A Mortuary Affairs Decontamination Collection Point (MADCP) is established whenever the threat of nuclear, biological, and chemical (NBC) warfare exists. The handling of contaminated remains is a three-phase process that consists of recovery, movement to the theater quality control station, and final verification of remains. Component and subordinate commands must address the following when planning MADCP operations:

- Capabilities.
- Supplies and equipment.
- Personnel.

- External support:
  - Transportation.
  - Engineer support.
  - Communications.
  - Decontamination (1 hour for recovery of each remains).
  - Security.
  - Medical support.
  - Maintenance.
  - EOD support.
  - Life support and/or personal services.

- Environmental factors:
  - Runoff of contaminated water.
  - Proximity to a populated area (i.e., civilian or military).

- Terrain considerations:
  - Proximity to a good road network.
  - Availability of landing zones and airfields.
  - Natural concealment and shading (e.g., small hills, dunes, buildings, trees).
  - Protection from the wind (i.e., should be located up wind of the contaminated area).

Remains Processing

Care and handling of deceased personnel begins with the search, recovery, tentative identification, and evacuation of remains.

Remains processing is the systematic process of searching for remains and personal effects, plotting and recording their location, and evacuating remains to a mortuary affairs facility. Unit commanders, at all levels, are responsible for the initial search, recovery, tentative identification, and evacuation of all deceased unit personnel within their area of operation. If a unit is unable to recover remains, the unit coordinates with the appropriate higher headquarters to request search and recovery support. Mortuary affairs personnel may assist units when required and if available.

The following forms will be filled out and delivered to the Joint Mortuary Affairs Office (JMAO):

- DD Form 1380, *Certificate of Death.*

- DD Form 2064, *Certificate of Death Overseas.*

- DD Form 894, *Record of Identification Processing—Finger Print.*

- DD Form 890, *Record of Identification Processing—Effects and Personal Data.*

- DD Form 1076, *Military Operations: Records of Personal Effects of Deceased.*

Search

The success of a search and recovery mission depends on a well-organized search pattern that is tailored to the situation. Strict discipline during the search must be maintained. This means that all search members must perform their duties and follow an established plan unless the tactical situation dictates otherwise.

Recovery

Units conducting battlefield recovery operations must take special precautions to preserve all items that might be helpful in establishing a tentative identification of remains. When performing recovery operations, units use every available means to protect all recovered remains. Units without human remains pouches can use ponchos, blankets, large plastic bags, or other suitable items to cover remains.

Safety and sanitation factors should also be considered. Disease can easily be transmitted from the remains to individuals handling the remains. Units should provide gloves and protective clothing for personnel conducting recovery operations and adequate washing facilities after the mission.

Units performing recovery operations must ensure that remains are safe to evacuate. Remains must be free of the risk of spreading harmful contamination, and they must have all unexploded ordnance and other hazardous items removed.

Tentative Identification

Identification of remains is critical. During recovery, units must ensure that identification tags and cards, if present, are not removed from the remains. Identification and other media must be protected from destruction by body fluids, weather conditions, and environmental factors. After these items are protected, they are secured to the remains. These items stay with the remains until inspected for identification value.

When recovering remains that are missing major portions, the immediate area is thoroughly searched for the missing portions. If the missing portions are not located, pertinent information on the incident is reported to the MACP when remains are evacuated. In areas having multiple remains and severed portions, no attempt is made to associate any individual portions found to a particular remains. Individual portions are tagged separately for evacuation. If fragmented remains are encountered, attempt is made to recover as much of the remains as possible. No piece or portion is considered too small. Information about the immediate surrounding area is reported to aid in identification.

Evacuation

Remains, portions, and personal effects are evacuated from the recovery site to a mortuary affairs facility using the most expedient manner of transport to prevent losing identification media due to decomposition of remains. Operational requirements may dictate the use of any available transportation assets; however, the use of medical and food bearing vehicles is not encouraged.

While awaiting transportation, remains are placed shoulder to shoulder on the ground and screened from public view and unauthorized persons. Remains are carried feet first. Remains are loaded feet first on vehicles and rotary-wing aircraft; head first on fixed-wing aircraft. Remains are placed in such a manner to prevent stacking and secured in such a manner to prevent shifting during movement. Individual(s) are assigned to accompany the remains and personal effects during evacuation. Remains are evacuated to the nearest MACP.

Interments

Emergency Burials

If the tactical situation requires a unit to move out of an area in an expedient manner without evacuating remains, a unit may request permission to conduct isolated interments. Permission is requested through command channels from the geographic combatant commander. Isolated interments are shallow graves constructed to prevent unattended remains in open areas. All personal effects and other identification media are intered with the remains. Identification tags or cards are not removed from remains under any circumstances. The interment site is marked in an easily distinguishable manner for future recovery teams.

The unit prepares and submits an incident report on the isolated interment of remains to the JMAO via higher headquarters as soon as time permits. Timely and accurate documentation from the unit is vital in ensuring that all remains are recovered and evacuated in a timely manner. At a minimum, the incident report should include 10-digit grid coordinates, the number of isolated graves, tentative identification of each remains, and markings of isolated graves.

Mass Burials

If tactical and logistical situations make it impossible to use preferred evacuation or emergency burial methods, mass or trench burials may be used to reduce the time between recovery and burial of remains. The JMAO in the theater, with the approval of the geographic combatant commander, gives permission for mass burials of casualties. If there are no mortuary affairs units in the area and contact with higher headquarters is lost, the senior officer in the area decides whether the remains should be buried in a mass grave or evacuated to the rear.

If a mass burial is required, the burial site may consist of any number of rows. Each row holds 10 remains, head to foot. The rows are approximately 70 feet long, 3.5 feet deep, and as wide as the earthmoving equipment blade (minimum of 2.5 feet). Ideally, rows should be side by side, but terrain may dictate otherwise. Once all burials have been completed in each row, the row is refilled. The beginning and ending of each row is marked with a metal stake, and a metal tag is securely affixed to each stake indicating the row number. If available, a global positioning system device is used to determine and record the location of each row.

Committal at Sea

Remains may be committed at sea when a death occurs aboard a ship at sea and prevailing operational constraints do not permit evacuation. If authorization from the appropriate Service component commander is granted to perform committal at sea, the ship's commanding officer appoints an officer in charge of the committal. The officer in charge conducts the committal in accordance with Army Regulation (AR) 638-2, *Care and Disposition of Human Remains and Disposition of Personal Effects*. Prior to committal, the ship's commanding officer ensures that remains are positively identified. The officer in charge is responsible for accurately recording all facts concerning the committal in the ship's log and for ensuring appropriate respect/honors are paid to the deceased. Personal effects are removed from the remains and examined for identification value. An identification case file, consisting of a statement of recognition from two individuals and a certificate of death signed by a medical officer, is established. After committal at sea, the officer in charge sends the JMAO the identification case file and a report detailing the committal, to include distribution of personal effects.

Disinterments

It is the geographic combatant commander's responsibility to ensure that all temporary interments are disinterred and the remains are returned to the continental United States for final disposition, if possible. The JMAO monitors, coordinates, and provides special guidance during disinterment operations.

It is the responsibility of the designated Service component commander to coordinate and supervise disinterment operations within the operational area. Service component commanders provide specialized equipment, personnel, and other support as necessary to accomplish the mission. The component commander's mortuary affairs office coordinates with the JMAO and obtains records and reports of burials required during disinterment. Remains are processed and sent to a collection point for further evacuation to a TMEP.

Chapter 5
Field Exchange Services

Marine Corps Community Services (MCCS) provides exchange services to Marines both in garrison and during deployments. The ability to provide field exchange services to deployed Marines increases morale. Exchange services while deployed are somewhat limited. The field exchange will not have an entire inventory of goods and services found at base/station exchanges, but there will be a wide variety of goods and services for Marines to choose from while they are in the field.

Exchange services provided to deployed units may vary from providing health and comfort packs, to periodic access to the base exchange or host nation equivalent, to establishing a tactical field exchange. Field exchange services consist of a tactical field exchange, a mobile field exchange, and ration supplement sundries packs (RSSPs). A tactical field exchange provides all the goods and services for the theater. A mobile field exchange is a vehicle that takes a limited amount of goods and services to troops within the theater who can't get to the tactical field exchange. An RSSP is a supplement to the tactical field exchange. It is issued to troops prior to the establishment of a functional tactical field exchange.

The establishment of a field exchange is based on three broad categories of deployments. The three categories and their retail requirements are as follows:

- Category I deployments are exercises with little opportunity for Marines to access MCCS assets. Limited retail and personal services operations exist; e.g., 1-day access to retail or exchange facility.

- Category II deployments are exercises up to 90 days in duration with some opportunity for Marines to access MCCS assets. Retail/personal services operations are expanded to include repeated access to base MCCS or host nation facilities. Units may request the establishment of a tactical field exchange.

- Category III deployments are exercises in excess of 90 days in duration and Marines have the opportunity to access MCCS assets. Retail/personal services operations are greatly expanded to include access to base MCCS or host nation service facilities.

Staffing Requirements and Responsibilities

The tactical field exchange platoon, organic to the FSSG, is composed of MOS-qualified 4130s and 4133s. It has a T/O and T/E designed to provide exchange services in a deployed environment. Staffing requirements are based on 1 officer or staff noncommissioned officer and 3 enlisted personnel to serve 1,000 customers. Two enlisted personnel are added per each additional 1,000 customers or portion thereof. This manning is based on operating a tactical field exchange for 9 hours a day plus an additional 3 hours a day for restocking and administrative requirements.

Prior to deployment, the MAGTF commander will review the stock assortment. Resupply, if necessary, will depend on availability of transportation (air/sea). Resupply will be through the parent exchange or Marine Corps supply system.

The director of the Personal & Family Readiness Division, MCCS, Quantico, VA, is responsible for worldwide planning and monitoring of tactical field exchanges. Within this division, the Retail Exchange Branch advises the director regarding policy and procedures in the operation and contingency planning of tactical field exchanges that are operating worldwide. The director may dispatch inspectors and advisors as needed to ensure proper operation and mission support. This division evaluates after-action reports, makes recommendations, and provides training and support to correct operational problems.

The tactical field exchange officer is directly responsible to the commanding officer, CSSE on matters pertaining to tactical field exchange operations. The tactical field exchange officer—

- Provides exchange operations in accordance with applicable directives.
- Is accountable for assigned tactical field exchange assets and inventory.
- Coordinates tactical field exchange movement and/or shipping requirements with the appropriate movement control agency.
- Coordinates with the camp commandant to identify sites from which to establish and operate tactical field exchanges.
- Oversees resupply to ensure adequate inventory is maintained.
- Ensures tactical field exchanges are staffed appropriately.
- Establishes mobile tactical field exchanges as required.

The CSSE G-1/S-1 has cognizance over the tactical field exchange and provides the supported tactical field exchange units with critical logistic and/or administrative support and services including the following:

- Facilities to house the tactical field exchange (tents or other structures).
- Class IV supplies.
- Tactical field exchange disbursing.

- Security.

- Transportation and materials handling equipment.

- Utilities and communications.

- Services to tactical field exchange personnel (i.e., billeting, subsistence, disbursing, postal, legal).

Planning Considerations

The tactical field exchange officer's initial focus is to provide Marines with personal demand items (i.e., clothing and hygiene products). Therefore, to provide quality and effective support, the tactical field exchange officer must be involved in the exercise/contingency operation's planning process. The tactical field exchange officer must have access to personnel numbers, geographic locations, estimated deployment duration, and conflict intensity in order to determine the required level of tactical field exchange support and to provide the supported unit with the tactical field exchange's operational requirements. The tactical field exchange officer must also take into account the three phases of deployment: predeployment, deployment, and post deployment.

Predeployment

During predeployment, merchandise is readied for shipment to the area of operations. The parent exchange or Army and Air Force Exchange Service prepares imprest funds to be used to purchase merchandise and operational equipment, and also prepares petty cash funds for tactical field exchange usage. The amount of merchandise required is based on the duration of the operation and the number of personnel supported. The merchandise is inventoried and containerized in preparation for shipment. The tactical field exchange officer assumes accountability for the shipment.

Deployment

During deployment, container(s) are shipped to the operational site(s). The tactical field exchange receives the merchandise and sets up and operates the retail store(s). When the operation is complete, the tactical field exchange is disassembled. All unsold merchandise and the remaining operating supplies/equipment are loaded into containers and shipped back to the parent exchange.

If the operation warrants the assumption of field exchange services by the Army and Air Force Exchange Service, the CSSE G-1/S-1 and the tactical field exchange officer develop a transition plan to turn over or to sell excess inventory to the Army and Air Force Exchange Service without a break in customer service.

Post Deployment

Post deployment concludes MCCS/tactical field exchange activity. All merchandise, supplies, and equipment are accounted for and returned to stock. All documentation, sales receipts, and returns are reconciled. The tactical field exchange officer is relieved of accountability unless large losses require an investigation.

Tactical Field Exchange

The tactical field exchange provides limited temporary support (basic health, hygiene, personal care needs, and snacks) to military personnel engaged in exercises, maneuvers, or contingency operations 30 to 90 days in duration. The tactical field exchange is provided by the CSSE (only class VI supplies required to stock the exchange is provided by the MCCS). The exchange platoon will bring all supplies and equipment necessary to support the MAGTF for a period of 30 days without resupply.

The deployed tactical field exchange activity is operated as a branch of the parent MCCS from which the unit is deployed. In the event a deployment is extended for a long period of time or in the case of extensive mobilization, exchange services are provided through the establishment of a Fleet Marine Force MCCS nonappropriated fund instrumentality. Funding for equipment, supplies, and resale goods are provided from mobilization contingency funds maintained by the Commandant of the Marine Corps. Requirements for this type of support must be referred to CMC (MW).

Mobile Tactical Field Exchange

Mobile tactical field exchanges can be an effective means of providing exchange support to remote and hard-to-reach units. Through coordination with the MAGTF G-3/S-3 and the movement control center, mobile tactical field exchanges can deliver health and comfort items to troops that otherwise would be unable to access a tactical field exchange due to their mission and geographic location.

Ration Supplement Sundries Pack

RSSPs are contingency items that provide the necessary gratuitous issue of health and comfort items to combat, combat support, and combat service support employed units until such time as exchange facilities can be established in the area of operations. RSSPs are considered class I (subsistence) supply for inclusion in supply blocks of deploying units because they provide only those items necessary to maintain the health of deploying Marines. Contingency plans to support RSSP supply block deployment requirements must exist and must be coordinated between the MAGTF commander and the MCCS director. Funding for RSSP items is accomplished by the deploying command.

Chapter 6
Security Support Services

This chapter briefly discusses the mission and functions of the military police in support of the MAGTF in an expeditionary environment. Security support as a subfunction of services relates primarily to the existence of an MP company in the H&S battalion of the FSSG, although each element of the MEF has an MP capability.

Military police are used for internal support, but the MAGTF commander can also use them as a force multiplier. They are capable of supporting MAGTF operations across the full range of military operations—peace, conflict, and war—and across the entire force continuum, both nonlethal and lethal force. But the MAGTF commander must judiciously prioritize limited MP assets to employ them effectively.

For detailed information on security support of the MAGTF, see MCWP 3-34.1, *Military Police in Support of the MAGTF*.

Mission

Military police can function as a training cadre to support the commander by providing instructions in nonlethal weapons use, antiterrorism/force protection, NEOs, civil unrest, and other security operations. Furthermore, military police perform specialized missions in areas of accident investigations, criminal investigations, employment of military working dogs, physical security, and corrections. These missions are performed during joint and multinational operations. In addition, military police enhance interoperability through liaison/coordination with joint, combined, host nation, and nongovernmental organizations.

Military police provide and enhance force protection during the execution of their mission, which inherently improves the unit's antiterrorism/force protection posture. They can advise the commander of the changing enemy and environmental situation and the probable impact each has on the commander's course of action in regards to antiterrorism/force protection. The criminal and tactical information gathered by the military police, Criminal Investigation Division, and Naval Criminal Investigative Service can assist in developing the MAGTF antiterrorism/force protection plan and in safeguarding all property and personnel in the area of operations.

Capabilities

Maneuver and Mobility Support Operations

At operational and tactical levels, effective use of the road network is typically a key component of movement. Military units and civilians will compete for space along limited road space causing congestion on road networks. Military police perform maneuver and mobility support operations to ensure maximum utilization of roads. They assist in the identification of primary and alternate routes, continuously monitor route conditions, and keep routes clear for vital military movements. Military police support maneuver, mobility, and survivability by expediting forward and lateral movement of combat service support resources and by conducting security missions.

Route Reconnaissance and Surveillance

Military police continually monitor and report the condition of the main supply route (MSR). This includes identifying restricting terrain along the MSR; determining the effects of weather on the MSR; identifying damage to the MSR; locating NBC contamination along the MSR; identifying enemy presence along the MSR; and identifying any alternate MSR. To perform this task, military police must perform the following actions.

MSR Regulation and Enforcement

Military police enforce the command's MSR regulations and traffic circulation plans to keep the MSR free for priority military movement. To expedite traffic on the MSR, military police use patrolling, traffic control points, roadblocks, checkpoints, holding areas, defiles at critical points, and temporary route signs. MP mobile teams also gather information on friendly and enemy activity.

Area Damage Control

Area damage control minimizes the effects of damage that has occurred in the area of operations; e.g., damaged or destroyed bridges, downed trees, urban rubble, contaminated road networks. Military police perform area damage control before, during, and after hostile actions or natural or manmade disasters. During damage control operations, military police employ traffic control measures to efficiently move military traffic, stragglers, and refugees through or around potential congestion points. Military police can also perform NBC detecting, reporting, and some local physical security when required.

Straggler and Dislocated Civilian Control

Military police, in concert with joint, allied, and host nation forces, divert refugees and other dislocated civilians from the MSR. They also identify stragglers and enable them to reunite with their units or make other disposition, as appropriate.

Information Collecting, Reporting, and Dissemination

While executing maneuver and mobility support missions, military police continuously collect intelligence information. This information is then reported to commanders, Marines, units, and other road users. As military police patrol an area, they gather information about the terrain, weather, and activities in the area of operation. This information is reported to the MAGTF G-2/S-2 for further analysis.

Area Security Operations

Military police conduct area security operations, typically in the rear area, to protect critical functions, facilities, and forces that support the combat forces. Military police perform the following during area security operations:

- Secure and protect lines of communications and routes into areas of operations, in rear areas in support of the combat operation, and during humanitarian assistance and peace operations.
- Secure designated critical assets.
- Detect enemy forces operating in the rear area.
- Conduct area of operations reconnaissance and surveillance.
- Conduct area damage control operations.
- Conduct intelligence collection and dissemination.

- Support NBC detection and reporting.

- Conduct area of operations security.

- Support antiterrorism operations.

- Conduct physical security advisories for base and installation defense.

- Conduct area of operations reconnaissance and surveillance.

- Conduct security of designated critical assets.

Primary Law and Order Operations

Military police conduct law and order operations as needed to extend the combat commander's discipline and control and to promote a lawful and orderly environment. Law and order operations include those measures necessary to—

- Enforce laws, directives, and punitive regulations.

- Conduct criminal investigations.

- Control populations and resources.

- Support customs operations.

- Perform police information operations; e.g., gathering information from criminal activities

- Employ military working dogs.

- Perform traffic enforcement and investigation.

- Perform joint, combined, and host nation police operations.

Chapter 7
Disbursing Services

Disbursing services provide the banking and currency support needed to pay U.S. military and other U.S. agency personnel. Disbursing services also include performing financial analyses and making recommendations that prepare the force to effectively use its fiscal resources. Effective financial support that spans the range of military operations provides the commander with the financial resources necessary for successful mission accomplishment.

Essential Elements of Financial Operations

Although each operation has its own unique set of financial parameters associated with its execution, all operations involve three essential elements of financial operations: provide financial advice and recommendations, support the procurement process, and provide disbursing support.

Provide Financial Advice and Recommendations

In order to provide the commander with accurate and complete financial advice and guidance, the economic impact of an operation must be analyzed as to its effect on the local economy in the area of operations and the ability of the local economy to support financial operations. The economic impact analysis includes, but is not limited to, how well the local infrastructure can support the required logistic and banking operations, how U.S. currency would affect the local economy, and which currencies or scrip should be used. If the economy is very rudimentary, such as a barter economy, it may provide only limited financial capabilities. Conversely, a highly developed, industrialized economy may be capable of providing a greater level of financial support.

Banking System

Highly developed economies can provide modern banking services such as local currency, checking accounts, and automated teller machines. These banks may also provide an inexpensive source of foreign currency or U.S. coin and currency.

Currency

Some currencies are not readily available on the open market. The availability of currency must be determined as early as possible in the planning process. The availability of currency can have a major effect on exchange rates and lead to large discrepancies between the official and black market exchange rates. Another consideration is the impact of a sudden influx of U.S. dollars on the local economy.

Other Negotiable Instruments

The culture and customs within the area of operations must be considered. For example, negotiable instruments such as personal checks, travelers checks, and credit cards are not acceptable in some countries.

Support the Procurement Process

Supplemental support of the logistic system and contingency contracting efforts are critical to the success of all operations. Supplemental support involves local purchasing of materials, supplies, and services. Locally contracted support is used to satisfy requirements for labor, materials, food, lodging, sanitation, and other services in the area of operations when they cannot be reasonably provided through established logistic channels or when the local procurement of materials and services will allow a commander to use scarce strategic lift and transportation assets for other purposes.

Contracting support is provided by a component's finance unit and involves paying for contracted services and supplies. A large percentage of the finance unit's contingency effort may be directed towards supporting the deployed contracting and purchasing effort.

Provide Disbursing Support

Disbursing support includes providing check cashing and foreign currency exchanges for U.S. military and civilian personnel, military pay and travel services for Marines, payments to local vendors, and other payments as required.

Check Cashing

While deployed, the disbursing officer provides check cashing services to Marine Corps personnel unless arrangements have been made with the ship or another Service's disbursing officer to provide these services. To some extent, and at the discretion of the disbursing officer, checks may also be negotiated for civilian personnel (federal employees only [contracted civilians included]). A commander may set limitations on check cashing privileges (e.g., monetary amounts, frequency) based on the availability of currency.

Foreign Currency Exchanges

Navy and Marine Corps disbursing officers may either purchase large amounts of foreign currency or hire contractors to perform currency exchange services. The disbursing officer is then able to perform foreign currency exchange services and ensure a fair exchange of U.S. dollars for local currency for Marines and Sailors.

Military Pay and Travel Services

Normally, the deployed disbursing officer manages the military pay and travel services of deployed Marines. The disbursing officer works in concert with the commanding officer to ensure that Marines are correctly paid for subsistence, imminent danger pay, hostile fire pay, career sea pay, family separation allowance, and per diem, as well as to properly credit Marines with the combat zone tax exclusion, when applicable. The disbursing officer also ensures that required adjustments, bonds, allotments, and special payments are made as directed.

Payments to Local Vendors

Working jointly with deployed contracting personnel, the disbursing officer is responsible for making authorized payments to local vendors in the area of operations.

Other Payments

The disbursing officer may be called upon to make other types of payments including those to noncombatant evacuees, prisoners of war, and compensation for damage caused by U.S. forces. These payments are subject to specific authority, circumstances, and limitations.

Pay Distribution During Deployment

The military pay system allows several different forms of pay distribution to prevent Marines and their dependents from suffering financial hardships during deployments. These include direct deposit, allotments, and split pay. The direct deposit program has pay deposited directly into a checking or savings account each payday, which eliminates the need for "hard checks." The allotment/bond authorization process allows a fixed amount to be sent to any person or institution each month. The split pay program allows a Marine to receive a fixed amount of money by cash or check each payday while deployed and the remainder of the Marine's pay is distributed to his financial institution through the direct deposit program.

Chapter 8
Civil-Military Operations Services

Civil-military operations (CMO) establish, maintain, influence or exploit relations between military forces, governmental and nongovernmental civilian organizations, and the civilian population in order to facilitate military operations and to consolidate and achieve U.S. operational objectives. It may also involve the military performance of activities and functions that are normally the responsibility of the local, regional or national government. CMO may be performed by designated civil affairs forces, by other military forces or by a combination of civil affairs and other forces. Civil affairs refers to designated active and reserve component forces and units specifically organized, trained, and equipped to conduct and/or support CMO. Civil-military activities are performed or supported by civil affairs units to enhance the relationship between military forces and civil authorities in areas where military forces are present. Civil affairs units provide functional specialty skills in areas that are normally the responsibility of the local, civil government.

CMO are an inherent responsibility of command in order to facilitate accomplishment of a commander's mission. The National Command Authorities (NCA) establishes a commander's authority to execute CMO. Joint force commanders (JFCs) plan and conduct CMO to facilitate military operations and help achieve political-military objectives derived from U.S. national security interests. CMO are applicable at the strategic, operational, and tactical levels of war.

Types of Civil-Military Operations

CMO are part of a larger subset of military operations known as military operations other than war (MOOTW). CMO include foreign humanitarian assistance, population and resource control, nation assistance operations, military civic action, emergency services, civil administration support, and domestic support operations. Foreign humanitarian assistance relieves or reduces the results of natural or manmade disasters or other endemic conditions. Population and resource control assists host-nation governments or de facto authorities in managing their population centers and resources in order to facilitate the JFC's mission. Nation assistance operations provide civil or military assistance to a nation by U.S. forces. Assistance is conducted based on mutual agreements between the nation and the United States. Military civic actions are intended to win support of the local population for the foreign nation and its military. Indigenous military personnel conduct these actions, while U.S. forces provide advice, supervision or technical support. Emergency services are activities that minimize the effects of disasters upon the civilian population, including the emergency restoration of destroyed or damaged vital utilities and facilities. Civil administration support is a unique action that is undertaken by U.S. commanders only when directed or approved by the NCA. Civil administration support consists of planning, coordinating, advising, or assisting those activities that reinforce or restore a civil administration that supports U.S. and multinational objectives in friendly or hostile territory. Domestic support operations supplement the efforts and resources of state and local governments and voluntary organizations in the event of a major disaster.

Even during war, a commander's CMO requirements can include activities more often associated with peacetime military operations, such as humanitarian assistance, noncombatant evacuation, and infrastructure recovery and restoration. CMO in war include, but are not limited to, the following:

- Population resource control measures to reduce, relocate or access civilians that may impede or otherwise threaten the success of ongoing and follow-on military operations.

- Command responsibilities to civilian population and resources. This includes recommendations to protect specific places and objects against attack; e.g., historic monuments, works of art, and places of worship.

- Resource procurement and distribution.

- Rear area and force protection.

- Disease controls.

- Initiation of restorative measures for civilian government or the establishment of a civil administration or military government necessary to stabilize, reinforce or reconstruct basic services and institutions.

- Support to DOD EPW and civilian internees programs.

Organization and Capabilities

U.S. Marine Corps commands, with reserve augmentation, have the capability to plan and conduct CMO. The Marine Corps does not maintain active duty civil affairs units. CMO activities are carried out using assets from within the MAGTF with reserve augmentation when available. CMO activities of U.S. Marine Corps civil affairs units are normally limited to the essential civil-military functions necessary to support the MAGTF's assigned missions.

U.S. Marine Corps reserve civil affairs units consist of two CAGs that augment the capability of the MAGTF. The CAGs, when activated, are capable of self-administration, but they require support from the MAGTF command element to coordinate logistic support. The 3d CAG is located at Camp Pendleton, California, under the operational control of Marine Corps Forces, Pacific (MARFORPAC). The 4th CAG is located at Naval Station Anacostia, Washington, D.C., under the operational control of Marine Corps Forces, Atlantic (MARFORLANT). Within the active force, the LSSS of the FSSG provides judge advocates with limited CMO training to support the MAGTF when reserves from the CAG are unavailable. During small-scale contingencies, organic MAGTF command personnel can conduct CMO.

The CAG provides special staff support to the MEF during the planning and execution phases of an operation. The CAG may be used across the full range of military operations. It plans, advises, coordinates, conducts, supervises, and evaluates activities between military and civilians in order to minimize mission interference and maximize civilian support for MAGTF operations. These activities include interaction between the MAGTF and the civilian population, host-nation civil police, U.S. civilian agencies, and a wide array of nongovernmental organizations. The CAG provides the MAGTF with information relative to local culture, customs, and traditions in order to facilitate military operations and reduce friction.

The CAG is organized to conduct CMO in support of the MAGTF mission. Normally, these activities do not include sustained military or nation building/rebuilding operations. Whenever the MAGTF operates in an inhabited area, civilian populations will impact operations. Civil affairs elements and personnel are economy of force measures intended to apply a few specially trained Marines to the MAGTF's planning and execution of operations. The civil affairs staff element serves to promote civilian actions and attitudes helpful to the MAGTF and to minimize actions and attitudes harmful to the MAGTF. Typically, the assigned civil affairs staff prepares assessments, agreements, and annexes that support the commander's plans and mission accomplishment. CMO activities always support the commander's legal and moral responsibilities under international and U.S. law.

External Civil Affairs Organizations

During operations, U.S. Marine Corps policy is to treat civilians humanely, reduce civilian interference, and ensure the United States meets its obligation under international law and U.S. policy. To achieve these policy objectives, the U.S. Marine Corps works closely with external organizations. Since CMO involve civil affairs specialists, U.S. military and nonmilitary elements, host nation or occupied nation elements, and international agencies, organizational coordination and cooperation are key to operational success. MAGTF commanders normally establish and maintain coordination with designated U.S. Army organizations to ensure consistency and facilitate transition of appropriate missions to U.S. Army responsibility.

Department of State

The Department of State (DOS) formulates and implements U.S. foreign policy. The DOS determines the extent that U.S. forces will intervene in a foreign country and the level of civil affairs support.

Department of Defense

DOD plans and conducts CMO as directed by the NCA and DOS.

U.S. Agency for International Development

The U.S. Agency for International Development (USAID) plans and supports long-term economic and social improvement programs. USAID is an independent agency under the policy direction of the International Development Cooperation Agency (IDCA). IDCA is part of the DOS. It supervises and directs foreign assistance programs.

U.S. Information Agency

The U.S. Information Agency (USIA) operates as the overseas U.S. information service. The USIA distributes information about the United States and publicizes U.S. military and civilian achievements in a foreign country. The President and various U.S. agencies receive information from the USIA.

United States Country Team

The U.S. country team consists of selected embassy representatives and other U.S. Government agencies operating within a country. The U.S. country team meets regularly with the U.S. ambassador and details current developments in the country and the current U.S. position. This organization's mission is to unify the coordination and implementation of U.S. policy within each foreign country. The U. S. country team usually includes, but is not limited to, the following people:

- Ambassador.

- Embassy staff (deputy chief of mission and political, economic, consular and administrative advisors).

- Military attaches.

- Military Assistance Advisory Group Representative.

- Senior USAID representative.

- Senior USIA representative.

- Senior military commander.

International Organizations

The U.S. country team works with international relief organizations to care for displaced civilians and victims of war. These organizations' efforts, combined with CMO, meet humanitarian obligations and reduce interference in military operations. If a host nation's or occupied nation's government is functioning, the introduction of international organizations is approved by the host or occupied nation.

Planning

Planning for and coordination of CMO activities facilitates mission accomplishment. CMO planning is based on national policy and reflects a variety of legal obligations. These obligations can include provisions of the U.S. Constitution, statutory law, judicial decisions, Presidential directives, departmental regulations and rules, and principles of international law, especially those incorporated in treaties and agreements applicable to areas where U.S. forces are employed. Specific guidance to assist combatant commanders in developing CMO plans and annexes is contained in the following:

- JP 3-07.1, *"Joint Tactics, Techniques, and Procedures for Foreign Internal Defense (FID),"* appendix E, contains CMO assessments and estimates for joint force commanders.

- JP 3-57, *Joint Doctrine for Civil-Military Operations*, appendix B, addresses the Presidential Decision Directive-56 (PDD-56), *Managing Complex Contingency Operations.* PDD-56 outlines planning procedures for complex contingency operations, including forming an executive committee to oversee interagency planning. Annex A to appendix B contains a sample political-military plan, which serves as a basis for joint force planning of a CMO.

Execution

The primary goal of MAGTF CMO is to support mission accomplishment. Normally, these operations do not include sustained military or nation rebuilding operations. MAGTF resources administratively and logistically support CMO planning and execution requirements. The MAGTF G-3/S-3 is the principal civil affairs staff advisor to the MAGTF commander. The civil affairs officer performs the duties of a special staff officer under the cognizance of the G-3/S-3.

Subordinate units plan and execute CMO activities when useful or as directed, and may be assigned their own supporting civil affairs elements or personnel. The officer in charge of the civil affairs unit is ordinarily the unit's senior Marine. Command and control of civil affairs units normally remains with the MAGTF commander under the purview of the G-3/S-3. Upon activation, the CAG assists the civil affairs officer with reconnaissance, survey, and liaison efforts.

At the MEF level, the civil affairs element may receive substantial direction from the JFC's civil affairs staff element or joint CMO task force, if organized. Coordination with all staff elements is important, but special consideration should be made to coordinate with public affairs and psychological operations staffs to support a common information operations campaign. The MAGTF commander may direct civil affairs forces to establish a civil-military operations center, which serves as focal point of coordination between the MAGTF and civilian planners.

Functional Capabilities

CMO functional capabilities can span the range of military operations, and they can include, but are not limited to, any combination of the following:

- Preparing CMO assessments, estimates, agreements, and annexes in accordance with Joint Operational Planning and Execution System (JOPES).
- Planning and coordinating CMO activities in coordination with logistic planners. For example—

  - Support for military forces from civilian resources.

  - Facilitate host-nation support and contracting to U.S. and/ or friendly forces.

- Support requirements and sourcing for civilian population and agencies.

- Assist, supervise or control self-supporting civilian sector operations.

- Assisting commanders, in coordination with the servicing staff judge advocate, in fulfilling lawful and humanitarian obligations to the civil or indigenous population.

- Minimizing local population interference with U.S. military operations.

- Supporting and coordinating CMO, such as humanitarian assistance and disaster relief.

- Assisting in the establishment and maintenance of a liaison or dialogue with indigenous personnel, agencies, and civilian organizations.

Responsibility

CMO responsibilities include, but are not limited to, the following:

- Identifying and developing CMO goals, concepts, and plans.
- Coordinating with existing civil affairs agencies and local authorities.
- Identifying and procuring civilian resources.
- Developing population and resource control measures to support rear area security plans and to maintain law and order.
- Coordinating MAGTF participation in military civic action programs for foreign internal defense operations.
- Coordinating with applicable U.S. agencies.
- Collecting, channeling, and controlling the local population.

- Preventing, controlling, and treating endemic/epidemic diseases of the local population.

- Preparing, issuing, and enforcing instructions governing conduct of the local government and population.

- Assisting in developing emergency civilian administration organizations.

- Safeguarding civilian rights, cultural items, and property.

- Assisting in identifying, recording, and processing of claims for compensation due to injury, death or property damage.

- Developing civil information, humanitarian assistance, and civic action programs.

Functional Tasks

The following lists identify the functional tasks performed by the MAGTF in support of CMO. Detailed information can be found in MCWP 3-33.1, *MAGTF Civil-Military Operations* (under development).

Public Health

- Coordinates the public health needs of the MAGTF, host nation, or occupied nation.

- Coordinates with appropriate joint staff agencies, MAGTF medical staff, and other personnel assets.

- Coordinates with civilian personnel and facilities to prevent or control outbreak of disease.

- Provides emergency evacuation or temporary hospitalization of sick, wounded, and injured civilians and coordinates their return to civilian hospitals.

- Distributes supplies and equipment to meet minimum civilian public health needs.

- Reestablishes indigenous public health resources and institutions.

Legal and Public Safety

- Develops and coordinates legal and public safety programs based on U.S. policy, MAGTF mission, treaties, and agreements.

- Establishes essential population and resource control measures required to maintain law and order and eliminate distrust and unrest.

- Prepares, issues, and enforces proclamations, directives, and instructions governing conduct of local officials, agencies, installations, and civilian population.

- Develops emergency civilian administrative organizations.

- Coordinates self-help projects and uses indigenous resources to reestablish local institutions and facilities.

- Negotiates, contracts, procures, and administers local labor, land, and other civilian resources to assist rehabilitation and construction efforts.

- Safeguards civilian rights, cultural items, and property.

Foreign Humanitarian Assistance

- Develops and executes foreign humanitarian assistance projects based on U.S. policy, MAGTF mission, treaties, agreements, and host-nation desires.

- Provides medical, dental, and veterinary care.

- Constructs rudimentary surface transportation systems.

- Conducts basic sanitation facilities and well drilling.

- Performs rudimentary construction and repair of public facilities.

Disaster Relief

- Alleviates the suffering of disaster victims.

- Provides humanitarian services and transportation of victims.

- Provides food, water, clothing, medical supplies, beds and bedding, fuel, temporary shelter, and technical personnel.

- Repairs essential services.

Civilian Containment and Control

- Minimizes civilian interference with MAGTF operations.

- Controls civilian movement while protecting both MAGTF operation and civilian interests.

- Handles movement and evacuation of dislocated civilians.

- Coordinates temporary shelter of dislocated civilians.

- Prepares for rearward movement of civilians.

- Establishes and directs refugee camps if large groups of civilians must be quartered for extended periods of time.

- Coordinates screening, medical care, sanitation, supply, transportation, and information dissemination requirements with appropriate agencies.

- Effects relocation of dislocated civilians as soon as possible.

Noncombatant Evacuation Operations

- Evacuates U.S. nationals and certain designated aliens from a foreign country where the host nation is either unable or unwilling to provide adequate protection.

- Plans, coordinates, and directs NEOs.

Dissemination of Civil Information

- Disseminates information to the host or occupied nation's local population that explains and supports the civil affairs mission.

- Coordinates with the U.S. Embassy, U.S. Government agencies, international organizations, and local officials.

- Plans and coordinates civil information activities within the framework of the U.S. country team, national, and MAGTF objectives and policies.

- Researches and analyzes the target audience and available media resources before beginning a civil information program.

- Provides the following information to civilians and the host or occupied nation:

  - Reason for military presence.

  - Refugee/displaced person movement routes and location of assembly points.

  - Availability of emergency health care, food, and water.

  - Sanitation requirements.

  - Maintenance of law and order; e.g., curfews.

  - Geographic areas and activities to avoid.

- Claims procedures and services.
- Requirements for U.S. contracts and employment.
- Rumor and enemy propaganda control.
- CMO programs and activities.
- Military operations disruptive to routine civilian activities.

Appendix A
Acronyms

ACE... aviation combat element
AR .... Army regulations

CAG .... civil affairs group
CJCSI ....Chairman of the Joint Chiefs of Staff Instruction
CMO..civil-military operations
COD .... cash on delivery
CSSE ....combat service support element

DOD .... Department of Defense
DOS.. Department of State

EPW .... enemy prisoner of war

FID ....foreign international defense
FSSG ....force service support group

GCE...ground combat element

H&S...headquarters and service

IDCA .... International Development Cooperation Agency

JAGInst .... Judge Advocate General instruction
JFC ....joint force commander
JMAO...Joint Military Affairs Office
JOPES ....Joint Operation Planning and Execution System
JP .... joint publication

LSSS...legal services support section
LSST ....legal services support teams

MACP ....Mortuary Affairs Collection Point
MADCP.......Mortuary Affairs Decontamination Collection Point
MAGTF... Marine air-ground task force

MARFORLANT .... Marine Corps Forces, Atlantic
MARFORPAC .... Marine Corps Forces, Pacific
MCCS .... Marine Corps Community Services
MCDP .... Marine Corps doctrinal publication
MCRP .... Marine Corps reference publication
MCWP .... Marine Corps warfighting publication
MEF .... Marine expeditionary force
MOOTW .... military operations other than war
MOS .... military occupational specialty
MP .... military police
MPS .... military postal service
MSR .... main supply route

NATO .... North Atlantic Treaty Organization
NBC .... nuclear, biological, and chemical
NCA .... National Command Authorities
NDP .... Naval doctrine publication
NEO .... noncombatant evacuation operation
NJP .... nonjudicial punishment

PDD .... Presidential Decision Directive

RLS .... request for legal services
RSSP .... ration supplement sundries pack

SJA .... staff judge advocate

T/E .... table of equipment
TMEP .... Theater Mortuary Evacuation Point
T/O .... table of organization

U.S. .... United States

USAID .... U.S. Agency for International Development

USIA .... U.S. Information Agency

Appendix B
References

Joint Publications (JPs)

3-07.1   Joint Tactics, Techniques, and Procedures
for Foreign Internal Defense (FID)

3-57   Joint Doctrine for Joint Civil-Military Operations

4-0   Doctrine for Logistic Support of Joint Operations

4-06   Joint Tactics, Techniques, and Procedures
for Mortuary Affairs

Department of Defense (DOD)

4525.6M   DOD Postal Manual, Vol I & II

Department of Defense Forms (DD Forms)

890   Record of Identification Processing—
Effects and Personal Data

894   Record of Identification Processing—Finger Print

1076   Military Operations: Records of Personal
Effects of Deceased

1380   Certificate of Death

2064   Certificate of Death Overseas

Naval Doctrine Publication (NDP)

4   Naval Logistics

Marine Corps Doctrinal Publication (MCDP)

4   Logistics

Marine Corps Warfighting Publications (MCWPs)

3.33.1   MAGTF Civil-Military Operations
           (under development)

3-34.1   Military Police in Support of the MAGTF

6-12   Religious Ministry Support in the USMC

Marine Corps Reference Publications (MCRPs)

4-11.8A   Food Services Reference

Army Regulation (AR)

638-2   Care and Disposition of Human Remains and
           Disposition of Personal Effects

Judge Advocate General Instructions (JAGInst)

5800.7c   The Manual of the Judge Advocate General
           (JAGMAN)

Presidential Decision Directive (PDD)

PDD-56   Managing Complex Contingency Operations